The Guide to Student Voice

For Students, Teachers, Administrators, Advocates, and Others.

student voice in schools

By Adam Fletcher

The Guide to Student Voice - 2nd Edition.

By Adam Fletcher.

ISBN-13: 978-0692217320

ISBN-10: 0692217320

© 2014 SoundOut

PO Box 6185
Olympia, WA 98507-6185 USA
soundout.org

(360) 489-9680

Cover and interior design by Victoria Bawn.

For information on how to request permissions to reproduce information from this publication, please visit SoundOut.org.

Suggested Citation
    Fletcher, A. (2014) *The Guide to Student Voice*. Olympia, WA: SoundOut.

Contents

Student Voice

Every student has a voice - but what does that mean?

Here are the basics of Student Voice.

What Is Student Voice?

More than ever, students, teachers, building leaders, advocates, and others are concerned with making schools better places by listening to students. This publication is about *Student Voice*.

Here are some important definitions.

- **Student Voice**—Any expression of any student about anything related to education and learning.

- **Improving Schools**—Action designed to make schools better places for students to learn.

- **Education**—A process of learning, either informal or formal or both.

- **Learning**—Any idea, thought, knowledge, or wisdom that is created, accessed, gathered, or known.

- **Student Engagement**—The sustained connection students can make to schools, learning, or education.

- **Meaningful Student Involvement**—A systematic approach for school transformation focused on engaging students as partners throughout the education system as designed by Adam Fletcher.

- **School Reform**—Any concerted effort to improve schools that relies on changing curriculum, procedures, assessments, or inputs. Also called school improvement or school transformation.

student voice in schools

Take Action Right Now!

Ready to do something with student voice right now? Here are 10 ways you can take action for student voice immediately.

1. **Read This Guide.** Student Voice is more than classes voting and meetings. Read this booklet and SoundOut.org for ideas!

2. **Brainstorm Change.** Your imagination is a terrible thing to waste! Write a list of different ways student voice can change your school right now.

3. **Teach About Student Voice.** Talk with your friends about how your school change, and ask for their ideas.

4. **Find An Adult Ally.** Create a learning partnership with an adult to help your efforts. Adult allies can make connections easier.

5. **Teach Others About Student Voice.** Hold a workshop, make flyers, and teach others about Student Voice.

6. **Create A Student Voice Plan For Your School.** Schools need Student Voice. Name how, when, where, and why that happens.

7. **Present Your Plan To School Decision-Makers.** Share your plan with teachers, principals, administrators, and the school board.

8. **Present Your Plan To Community Decision-Makers.** Present to neighborhood associations, businesses, and government leaders.

9. **Organize.** Find allies by sharing Student Voice whenever you can. Work together, determine a goal and take action!

10. **Find Allies Online.** Look online through websites like SoundOut.org. It's just a matter of asking people to connect!

Ready to learn more? Want to dig in?
This booklet is meant to help you bring
student voice with power!

5 Ways Student Voice Changes Schools

1. **Engaging Student Voice Can Improve Learning.** When Student Voice is purposefully infused in classrooms, *all* students become engaged learners. Sharing their opinions, learning from their own lives, and finding themselves in the curriculum all reflect Student Voice.

2. **Engaging Student Voice Can Improve School Climate.** The school climate is made of the ways students, teachers, and other people in the school feel and act towards each other. Student Voice can best affect school climate through democratic activities, free speech, and systematically engaging Student Voice, also called Meaningful Student Involvement.

3. **Engaging Student Voice Can Improve Teaching.** When adults engage Student Voice, students can feel there is a real investment in their education from a caring adult. Students can share their ideas, opinions, wisdom, action, and knowledge in many ways—read the rest of this guide for some.

4. **Engaging Student Voice Promotes Lifelong Learning.** Learning to learn is a something all students should do. All students should build their understanding about education, the purpose of schooling, the course of the education system, and lifelong learning. From kindergarten through graduation, teachers can teach students about learning.

5. **Treat Student Voice As A Living, Breathing Approach That Must Keep Evolving.** Will Rogers once said, "Even if you're on the right track you'll get run over if you don't move." We live in a world of transition and change; students change with the times, and often with the days. Engaging Student Voice in schools should be a moving target that reflects the world. Use new methods, teach new approaches, and constantly demand more of students and educators.

How Do Students Start Changing Schools?

1. <u>Learn About Schools</u>. Learn how the school system works and about the education policies and laws that apply.

2. <u>Partner With Adults</u>. Find at least one adult who will be your partner. A teacher, parent, principal, counselor, or someone else.

3. <u>Share Successfully.</u> Communicate your student voice in ways that others—including students and adults—can easily understand.

Who Is Student Voice For?

Research shows that when it was actually heard, Student Voice can help a lot of people throughout education. Here are some of them.

- **Student Voice Is For ALL Students.** All students have ideas, opinions, experience, knowledge, and wisdom that should be heard throughout the education system. Students who dropout, get low grades, underperform on tests, and bully should be heard as much as students who excel in schools, join student government, and earn awards from teachers.

- **Student Voice Is For ALL Teachers.** Since every student can share Student Voice, every teacher can benefit from it. Classroom teachers of all grades and subjects, special education teachers, and substitute teachers can discover the depth, purpose, and value of Student Voice.

- **Student Voice Is For Support Staff.** Librarians, counselors, coaches, and every other adult who supports students in schools can benefit from engaging Student Voice.

- **Student Voice Is For School Leaders.** Principals, headmasters, and other school leaders can infuse Student Voice in building leadership. Beyond simply informing school leaders, students can co-lead as partners.

- **Student Voice Is For Parents.** When they listen to their children of any age, parents can make more informed decisions and stay in tune with what their students are experiencing in schools.

- **Student Voice Is For Education Leaders.** Elected and appointed school board members, superintendents, and others can engage Student Voice to get authentic perspectives on K-12 schools today.

Student voice benefits everyone in education, not just the students.

Places for Student Voice

When you understand who is involved in the education system, you can understand how, where, when, and why school happens the way it does. This can let you influence decision-making, guide decision-makers, and become as *real* decision-makers in your own rite. This will make you an owner of your education, and when you own education, learning and leading in schools becomes better for everyone.

Student voice happens in all these places, and more. Do you want to know exactly where Student voice can happen in schools? Here's a list. Each place is unique and powerful, and when done right should show the power and effectiveness of Student voice.

Places for Student Voice

- **Student Voice Happens In Teaching**—Student voice happens all the time in classrooms. It is students talking to each other and the teacher, and so much more. Students' behavior, attitudes, and actions are also forms of student voice. The student sharing their life experience is sharing student voice, just like the student cheating on a test or bullying.

- **Student Voice Happens In Class Evaluations**—When students evaluate themselves, their teachers, their peers, the curriculum, physical classroom, or other parts of the school, they're meaningfully involved. Its easy to incorporate listening to student voice this way- but its not meaningful until action comes from it.

- **Student Voice Happens In School Boardrooms**—Students can present ideas, share concerns, and sit through school board meetings just like adults. When school boards involve students as representatives of their peers, they are listening to student voice. Full-voting positions on school boards ensures student voice has power and not just presence.

- **Student Voice Happens In School Planning**—Student voice in school planning includes creating school culture, planning school activities and operations, promoting school improvement, and designing the physical building.

- **Student Voice Happens In Hallways**—When a student graffitis on the wall "Mrs. Jones Sux!", they're sharing student voice. So are students who gossip, form cliques, and share lockers. Student voice happens informally throughout schools all the time, with/without adult supervision and/or approval.

- **Student Voice Happens In School Research**—Students who research their schools examine learning, behavior, funding, policies, and more for efficacy and purpose. Both sharing and collecting student voice, involving students meaningfully as school researchers can help identify gaps and secure data in ways that many adult researchers cannot.

- **Student Voice Happens In School Protests**—Student-led school advocacy can include school protests. When adults don't involve students in meaningful ways throughout the school system, students may feel compelled to make their voices heard by adults. This is one way how that happens.

- **Student Voice Happens In Making Policy**—More than one student voice campaign in the 1960s had the motto, "Nothing about me without me," and they were frequently talking about education policy-making. Always the target of formal decisions in schools, students are rarely engaged in the processes that affect them most.

- **Student Voice Happens In School Reform**—Where adults stand on either side of a school building a poke sticks at each other in the name of improving schools, they have frequently lost sight of students. They do this because they haven't engaged students as partners in school reform. Student voice can have a role when students share what they think about schools and how they can improve; students can be engaged as partners when they have substantive roles in school reform activities.

- **Student Voice Happens Afterschool**—Student voice can happen throughout afterschool activities, both educational and recreational, in school and otherwise. Students can plan, evaluate, facilitate, research, advocate, and more for the activities designed to serve them.

student voice in schools

- **Student Voice Happens In Clubs**—Clubs and other extracurricular activities give the appearance of being an appropriate outlet for student voice. However, without earning credit for their contributions or otherwise being acknowledged for their contributions, and with the intentional positioning of student voice as irrelevant to school day learning, students may learn from clubs that their voices are best tokenized if not entirely ignored.

- **Student Voice Happens In Teaching**—Student voice in teaching means giving students opportunities to share their experiences, ideas, knowledge, questions, and action. That can happen through curriculum planning and delivery, as well as evaluation and reflection.

- **Student Voice Happens In School Year Planning**—Looking over the scope of learning activities gives students insight into how education operates. Student voice can inform and drive school year planning and provide a collaborative basis for Student/Adult Partnerships by giving students purpose in schools.

- **Student Voice Happens In Sports**—The first occurrence of the phrase "student voice" in my research emerges from a 1956 newspaper article on college sports at Columbia University. Since then sports in elementary and secondary education have taken root, and adults' responses to student voice have varied. Students can share a lot, including essential play information and more.

- **Student Voice Happens In Educator Hiring**—Hiring adults to work with students throughout the education system is generally done by adults. However, student voice in educator hiring, administrator hiring, and the hiring of school support staff can help foster environments that are more responsive, safe, and supportive for students *and* adults.

- **Student Voice Happens In Political Rallies**—Engaging student voice in political rallies has to extend beyond simply using young people to decorate adult causes. Propping up a student and telling them what to say is not student voice.

- **Student Voice Happens In Discipline**—When students help make classroom guidelines, school policies, and district regulations, student voice can happen through discipline. Student courts are another approach, as is having students engaged in deciding remediation and conflict resolution.

- **Student Voice Happens In Curriculum Planning**—Curriculum planning can be made richer and more effective with student voice. By participating as partners, students can help decide topic areas, curricular approaches, teaching methods, and other essential parts of the process. Student voice can be most effective in equal partnerships through regular curriculum committees, as well as individual teacher planning.

- **Student Voice Happens In District Offices**—District, regional education units, and state education agencies can engage student voice throughout their processes. Grant planning, delivery, and evaluation; policy creation and evaluation; school improvement planning; building assessment; and many more locations throughout education administration are places for student voice in district offices. **Student Voice Happens In Technology**—Student voice in education technology begins with simply listening to students in teaching. Student voice can happen by having students teach students and teachers about technology; students maintain and develop educational technology infrastructure in schools; and students design ed tech policies on the building, district, state, and federal levels.

- **Student Voice Happens In Teacher Training**—When students teach teachers about youth culture, student rights, learning styles, and other topics important to them in schools, student voice can be infused in teacher training.

- **Student Voice Happens In The Principal's Office**—Student voice in the principal's office has an important role in decision-making on the personal level and affecting the whole student body. In addition to advocating for themselves, student voice can help building leaders to affect school improvement through Principal Advisory Councils and other formal and informal mechanisms.

- **Student Voice Happens In Grant Evaluations**—Evaluating the efficacy of the grant-making designed to serve them positions student voice to impact learning beyond the classroom. Adults gain important skills and

> ## DECISIONS TO MAKE WITH STUDENT VOICE
>
> ★ Decide number of employees in schools
> ★ Select textbooks and materials
> ★ Hire new principals and teachers
> ★ Consult on curriculum
> ★ Identify what topics should be taught
> ★ Suggest how teaching happens
> ★ Select which topics teachers teach
> ★ Determine classes students can take
> ★ Choose how time will is used
> ★ Review how school buildings are used
> ★ Make classroom management policies
> ★ Create extracurricular activities
> ★ Budget how funds are to be spent
> ★ Plan teacher in-service days

HOW STUDENT VOICE CAN HELP WRITE CURRICULUM

★ Propose a series of topics or themes.

★ Ask questions designed to make students and teachers talk to each other.

★ Keep focused on learning goals.

★ Create a menu of activities students can pick from to figure out how they want to teach class.

★ Make assessments that can help students learn more.

★ Help students thinking critically and demonstrate understanding about what they've written.

★ Join students and teachers together to reflect on how the curriculum is delivered.

perspectives, as well as energy for implementation, while students gain important understanding about the purpose of funding for their learning.

• **Student Voice Happens In School Budgeting**—Engaging students as partners in complex education budgeting gives student voice a purposeful outlet to affect the school system. Educators and administrators can gain important insight to the effectiveness of decision-making and implementation.

• **Student Voice Happens On Playgrounds**—When student voice has an intentional role in playgrounds, playing and conflicts have purpose that can be captured for learning. Observing, but not facilitating, playground interactions allows adults in schools to help students navigate where and how to use their voice appropriately in interpersonal relationships, as well as school-wide applications.

• **Student Voice Happens In School Culture**—The attitudes, policies, and structures of education may change when student voice happens. Culture includes the spoken and unspoken norms in a school, as well as the beliefs, ideas, actions, and outcomes of students and adults. Engaging student voice deliberately can improve all these things for everyone in education.

• **Student Voice Happens In The Cafeteria**—Student voice in the school cafeteria extends far beyond student complaints about food quality and fighting. Students are rallying schools to provide healthy choices, improve menu selection and pricing, and eliminate competitive foods from their buildings.

• **Student Voice Happens In Building Design**—Student voice can be engaged throughout building design processes and in all grade levels. From design to redesign to improvement to reconstruction, students can inform, co-design, and implement building planning in all areas.

• **Student Voice Happens In The News**—It's increasingly popular to quote students in education articles. Student voice also includes student-created articles for mainstream websites and newspapers, student-led video, school twitter feeds, and other news distribution channels.

• **Student Voice Happens In School Committees**—Student voice on committees can happen within school buildings, at district and state levels, and at the federal level. Students can participate as full partners in policy-making, grant distribution, curriculum selection, teacher hiring and firing, and more.

soundout
student voice in schools

Questions to Ask Yourself

- What is important to me in education?
- How do I feel connected to my school right now: Connected? Apathetic? Needed? Ignored? Useful? Well-Recognized? Why?
- How do I feel when I know I'm needed by something or someone?

Action Steps

1. Make a list of places in schools you can change with Student Voice.
2. Determine the strengths and needs of those places.
3. Decide how you can use your strengths to improve that place.
4. Help others figure out why they should care about Student Voice in that place.
5. Brainstorm ways you can work together to spread the word.
6. Take action!

Points to Remember...

The number of places where student voice has an essential role in schools is countless. Three important things to remember:

- Student Voice is not the same as student engagement or Meaningful Student Involvement.
- Student Voice is the *beginning* of engaging students—*not* the end.
- Meaningful Student Involvement yields the greatest outcomes for Student Voice.

student voice in schools

Student Voice in Education

If Student Voice is always present, why do we need to focus on it? Here are some important reasons we should consider.

Student Voice in Learning

Student Voice, which is any expression of any student about anything related to education and learning, can be infused into classrooms to help students learn better.

It can be easy to misbelieve that Student Voice is just about letting students have a say in what, how, why, when, or where they're taught. That is not true. Student Voice is *any* expression of students. Here are some points to guide your understanding about Student Voice and learning.

8 Key Points about Student Voice in Learning

1. **All Student Voice Matters.** Every expression of students matters in their education, including positive or negative ones.

2. **Every Learning Relationship Matters.** Every time a student interacts with a teacher, other students, and other adults affects learning.

3. **Students Aren't Incomplete.** All parts of a student's life have learning embedded in them that can and should be acknowledged in school.

4. **Total Responsibility Is Shared.** Students and educators *share* total responsibility for learning *and* teaching, no matter the setting.

5. **Students Know Things.** The unacknowledged expertise, wisdom, and knowledge of students should fill classrooms, and educators are missing out when they don't tap into it.

6. **Equity, Not Equality.** Students and adults do not have the same knowledge, experience, or ability. Appropriate adjustments should be made for students to become meaningful partners throughout the education system.

7. **It's About Learning, Teaching, And Leadership.** Students need opportunities for applied learning in order to affect schools, and what better way than integrating Student Voice throughout schools?

8. **Student Voice Requires More Than Just Talking.** There's a cycle that has to happen for Student Voice to actually matter in schools. It features adults Listening to Students; Validating what is said; Authorizing change to happen; Mobilizing students and adults and taking action; and then Reflecting on what's happened. See the following Cycle of Engagement for more information about that.

student voice in schools

What Student Voice Does in Learning

Student Voice can show...

- Do students feel teachers really care?
- Are teachers really trying to understand how students feel?
- Do teachers seem to know if something is bothering students?
- Do students in this class actually respect their teachers?
- Do students behave the way teachers want them to?
- Is this class actually doing work and not wasting or just filling time?
- Is behavior in a class under control?
- Do teachers explain difficult things clearly?
- Do teachers have good ways to explain topics in class?
- Do teachers successfully teach different types of learners?
- Do teachers know when a class understands, and when they do not?
- How much do students learn in each day?
- Do students learn to correct their mistakes?
- Do teachers let students give up when the work gets hard?
- Do teachers accept nothing less than students' full effort?
- Do students like the ways they learn?
- Do teachers make lessons interesting?
- Do teachers make learning enjoyable?
- Do teachers respect student ideas and suggestions?
- Do teachers want students to share their thoughts?
- Can students speak up and share their ideas about class work?
- Do teachers give students time to explain their ideas?
- Do teachers check to make sure students understand what they are teaching?
- Do teachers work with students to help students understand how to improve?
- Do students learn from what they do wrong on assignments?
- Do students see themselves and their lives in what they're learning?
- Are teachers and students stuck in traditional relationships, or are actively creating student/adult partnerships that transform schools and lives?

SoundOut
student voice in schools

15

Student Voice and Power

With classrooms, hallways, and schools filled with Student Voice, it's important to know that classrooms are just one place where it is at work. However, there is a difference between being heard and taking action. This section explores what happens when student voice meets power.

Student Voice + Power =
Meaningful Student Involvement

Student Voice happens everywhere all the time, and schools need more than that. Teachers, principals, counselors, coaches, cafeteria workers and janitors think they already have all students figured out because they've always heard Student Voice—even if they ignored it!

Adam Fletcher's Cycle of Engagement

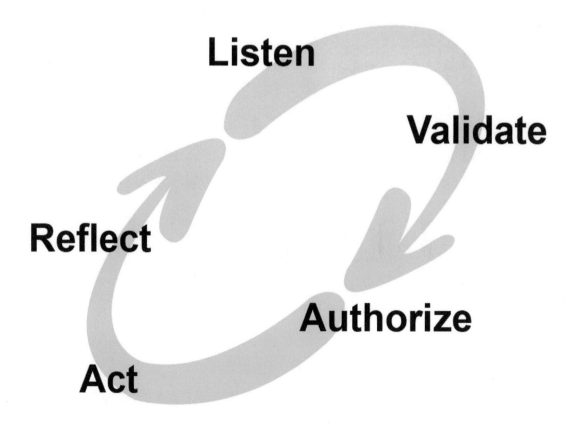

student voice in schools

16

Student Voice doesn't become powerful through some magical formula or mysterious bargain with students—but, it doesn't just happen, either. After working with thousands of students in hundreds of schools, I began seeing a process where student voice becomes powerful. I call it the Cycle of Engagement.

- Listen To Student Voice—Student Voice becomes powerful first by being listened to. Providing space a platform for Student Voice to be heard can be challenging. Listening to Student Voice can happen in personal conversations, classroom discussions, agenda items in meetings, or through written reports and studies.

- Validate Students—When students speak, it's not enough for adults to just nod your head. Validating students does not mean automatically agreeing with them, either. It is important to offer students sincere comments, criticism, or feedback. Disagreeing with students allows young people to know that adults actually hear what was said, that they thought about it, and that adults have their own knowledge or opinion they think is important to share with students. Students must know that education isn't about autonomous authority, and that a chorus of voices inform learning and leading schools.

- Authorize Student Action—If Student Voice has power, it has to have ability. Ability comes from experience and knowledge. Providing students with authority means going beyond traditional roles for students in classrooms by actively providing the training and positions they need in order to affect change. It is essential that adults provide students with the opportunities they need to be authors of their own narratives.

- Mobilize Students—Moving students from passive recipients to active learners and leaders throughout the education system requires students taking action to improve schools. Mobilizing students in positions of new authority allows them to affect cultural and systemic educational transformation, and encourages adults to acknowledge students as partners.

- Reflect On Action—Student Voice does not happen in a vacuum. Adults and students should take responsibility for learning through Student Voice by engaging in critical reflection and examining what was successful and what failed. Students and adults can also work together to identify how to sustain and expand the Cycle of Engagement by effectively returning to *Listening to Student Voice* again.

This Cycle isn't just something that adults do to students, either. It is *extremely* powerful when students do each step with each other. Individually, these steps may be happening in schools right now. However, when they do happen it is rare that they are connected with school improvement, and even less likely, connected with one another.

The connection of all the steps in this Cycle is what makes student-adult partnerships meaningful, effective, and sustainable.

Student Voice can become truly powerful when it is engaged through the Cycle. When that happens it becomes Meaningful Student Involvement. Power happens when a person is aware of their ability to make things change in the world around them. Meaningful Student Involvement makes change the purpose of Student Voice. Meaningful Student Involvement reflects:

- High-Bar Student Voice. Students are capable of much more than they've been given credit for traditionally, and engaging them as partners throughout education shows how far that goes.

- Student/Adult Partnerships. Giving students full control over schools is unrealistic and impractical. However, today adults generally act like students are incapable of leading and transforming education. Meaningful Student Involvement is the balance between students and adults throughout schools.

- Learning Through Change. Instead of focusing on keeping things the same, Meaningful Student Involvement intentionally shakes things up. Student Voice shouldn't reassure that things are going great in schools; it should serve as a loud call that things need to change. That happens through Meaningful Student Involvement.

- Transformed Systems, Cultures, And People. Instead of relying only on new curriculum, different assessments, or dynamic teaching, Meaningful Student Involvement starts *anywhere* in education and goes everywhere.

What Makes Involvement Meaningful?

When students and adults are partners in schools, that's Meaningful Student Involvement. When students and adults see each other as powerful, positive allies throughout education, that's Meaningful Student Involvement.

Student Voice becomes powerful when it has these six characteristics:

- School-Wide Approaches—All students in all grades are meaningfully involved throughout their education, including their learning experiences, classroom management, interactions with peers and adults throughout the school, and ongoing throughout their educational careers.

- High Levels Of Student Authority—The ideas, knowledge, opinions and experiences of students are validated and authorized through adult acknowledgement of students' ability to improve schools.

- Interrelated Strategies—Students are incorporated into ongoing, sustainable school improvement activities in the form of learning, teaching, and leadership in schools.

- Sustainable Structures Of Support—Policies and procedures are created and amended to promote meaningful student involvement throughout schools.

- Personal Commitment—Students and adults must acknowledge their mutual investment, dedication, and benefit, visible in learning, relationships, practices, policies, and school culture.

- Strong Learning Connections— Classroom learning and student involvement are connected by classroom credit, ensuring relevancy for educators and significance to students.

The Difference Between...

Student Voice &	Meaningful Student Involvement
* Any expression of a student about education	* Student voice is part of Meaningful Student Involvement
* Happens every where, all the time	* The WHOLE school changes
* Doesn't require change by adults	* Adults and students change
* Doesn't require change by students	* Designed for the whole school system
* May or may not change anything	* Promotes deep commitment by students and adults

What Difference Does It Make?

You should know about Meaningful Student Involvement because it can *realistically* make student voice a part of the very fabric of schools. As the system stands right now, there's no way every student can be engaged throughout all parts of education. Teachers aren't changing fast enough, lawmakers wouldn't consider making it a law, and researchers aren't making their case fast enough. Meaningful Student Involvement gives adults in schools and students a logical, systematic way to engage students as partners.

Presenting workshops across the country through the 2000s, I heard one question hundreds of times:

"Why does student voice matter?"

Sometimes it was a rhetorical question and sometimes it was mean, but usually it was simply honest. Educators want to know what advantages there are to engaging students as partners throughout education. Following is a simple summary of reasons why Student Voice matters, and how it transforms schools. Every point here is from research literature, and you can find the citation list online at soundout.org/library.html.

General Tips for Creating Student/Adult Partnerships

★ Build a team of students and adults working together to promote Student Voice and Student/Adult Partnerships.

★ Mutual respect is essential. Without basic respect, there's no trust, and without trust, Student/Adult Partnerships can't exist.

★ Back up students with care and support: Some young people don't know failure isn't the end. They need encouragement and support to learn from mistakes.

★ Learn through action: Structure all activities with the Cycle in order to learn from experience and apply new learning to life.

★ Establish and maintain mutual accountability: Students need to experience being accountable to others and holding others accountable in appropriate ways too.

★ Set responsibilities at appropriate levels—too high, failure guaranteed; too low, insulted intelligences and bored people.

★ Provide equitable training for students to learn enough to participate fully, given what adults in education already know.

★ Listen to each other!

Research shows...

- Student Voice Is About Learning—Engaging students as partners may be the most powerful lever available to improve student learning in schools.

- Student Voice Is About Teaching—Student involvement throughout the teaching process, from planning to evaluating teachers, can increase teacher efficacy, self-confidence, and retention.

- Student Voice Is About Improving Schools—Involving students can significantly improve adult leadership throughout education.

- Student Voice Is About Youth Development—Students can become more effective learners when their emotional, intellectual, and social needs are met.

- Student Voice Is About School Culture—The attitudes, policies, and structures of education may change when students are engaged as partners in schools.

- Student Voice Is About Diversity—Embracing a diversity of perspectives can make Student/Adult Partnerships the most significant tool in the school improvement toolbox.

- Student Voice Is About Integrity—Educators have an ethical responsibility to engage students as partners.

- Student Voice Is About Civic Engagement—When students are partners throughout schools they can learn about the necessity of active citizenship in their schools and throughout their lives.

- Student Voice Is About The "Bottom Line"—Engaging students as partners can help schools save money while meeting the rigorous demands facing public education systems.

Maybe the most important factor to Meaningful Student Involvement is that it just feels right. Students, teachers, administrators, researchers, professors, parents... the rooms of people attending SoundOut workshops come from a lot of different places and do a lot of different work that affects education in many different ways. However, by the end of any of our workshops they usually agree that, at the very least, it feels right. That important identification lays a foundation to work from, and the important findings detailed above support it.

student voice in schools

The Education System

How can we ensure Student Voice doesn't get lost in the sea of people involved in schools? By thinking strategically about where, how, and what students can do.

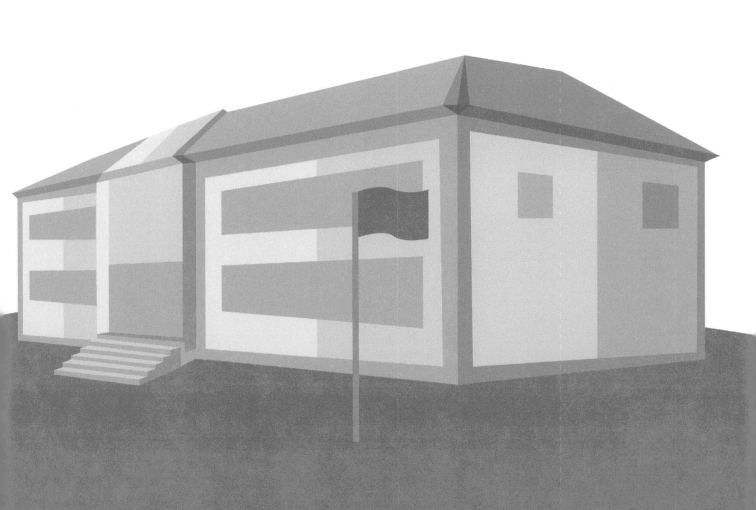

Education Is A System

There are many places in the U.S. education system where Student Voice can happen. They are different according to the state and city you live in, and whether you attend private or public schools.

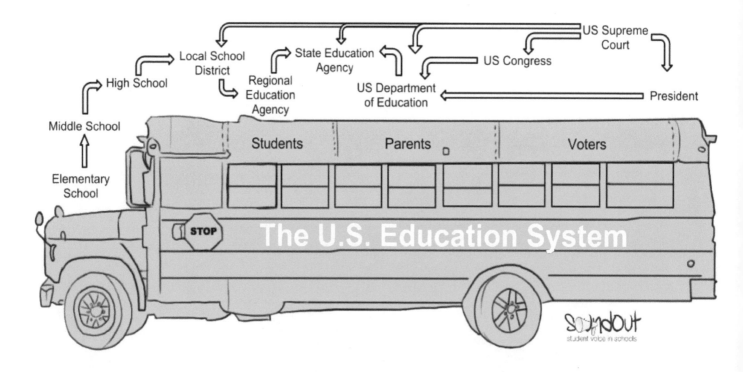

To make sure Student Voice is most effectively engaged, students should learn about the education system they participate in. The education system is the structure we rely on to ensure people learn essential lessons to be successful members of society. It includes everyone from students to parents, teachers to principals, district superintendents to state school boards, and several parts of the federal government.

Places for Student Voice in the Public Education System

Each of these places in the education system is occupied by a person.

The following section explores who they are.

1. Elementary, middle, and senior high schools

2. Local school districts (Called LEAs, or Local Education Agencies, as well as parishes, counties, or city governments)

3. Regional education agencies

4. State education agencies (Called SEAs, or State Education Agencies. May include state education leader offices)

5. U.S. Department of Education (Operated by the U.S. Secretary of Education)

6. U.S. Congress (Includes the U.S. House of Representatives and the U.S. Senate)

7. U.S. Supreme Court

8. White House (Office of the U.S. President)

CRITICAL QUESTIONS FOR ADULTS

★ Are your expectations for Student Voice reasonable and positive?

★ What do you first think of when you think about Student Voice in your own education setting?

★ Are you excited about the possibilities?

★ Are you considering the benefits and value of student contributions?

★ What kind of students do you want to engage?

★ Can you listen seriously to what students have to say even though they may not express their ideas in similar ways as you?

★ Have you clearly let students know your expectations for their participation?

★ Have you done your best to provide students with the resources they need to reach the set goals?

★ Have you picked a time when students are available to join in?

★ What kind of time commitment are you expecting? Will students be able to fit activities in with other commitments?

★ Have you provided teachers with enough information to give students credit for learning while sharing Student Voice?

Roles in Education

Getting clear on who is involved in schools is not always clear.

ROLES IN THE EDUCATION SYSTEM

Voters
President
Congress
Supreme Court
Federal Secretary of Education
Federal Department of Education
State Governor
State Legislature
State Supreme Court
State School Board
State Education Leader
State Administration
Regional Administration
District School Board
District Superintendent
District Administration
Principal
Assistant Principal
Teachers
School Support Staff (Counselors, Nurses, etc.)
Paraprofessionals
Parents
Adult Volunteers
Student Leaders
Students

In order to affect schools, you can build your understanding of how decision-making in schools works. The above positions represent the typical "flow" of decision-making affecting students in public schools. Different people may exert different kinds of influence in every decision. Each person is not guaranteed a place "at the table" (most here often are excluded). Following is a summary of everyone who *might* be involved.

student voice in schools

Roles That Can Benefit From Student Voice

Each of these roles can include student voice; few meaningfully involve students. Following are descriptions of each role, and how Meaningful Student Involvement can happen with them:

1. Students—All students everywhere, in every grade and every school, should experience Meaningful Student Involvement every day. Individual students determine whether they're meaningfully involved. You are in ultimately in charge of your own education because you can actively choose whether or not you are going to actively participate and learn in schools.

2. Peers—Younger and older students actively and passively influence other students' decision-making. This can be meaningful if its done intentionally to make schools better.

3. Student Leaders—Many schools have active programs that draw out "traditional student leaders" by identifying certain skills or abilities students have. Despite having a range of abilities, these student leaders are mostly focused on activities that affect students only. However, a growing number of student leaders have an increasing amount of ability to affect the whole education system. There are also "nontraditional" student leaders whose influence over their peers' decision-making has not been acknowledged in school.

4. Parents—Guiding children is one of the most important jobs of parents; this is especially true in schools. Parents can also passively or actively decision-making.

5. School Support Staff/Paraprofessionals/Adult Volunteers—Secretaries, adult tutors, coaches, librarians, classroom assistants, and parent representatives may influence student decision-making. Paraprofessionals are people who are hired to work in schools to help students and teachers be successful.

6. Teachers—Everyday students are subjected to a range of decisions made by teachers about grading, curriculum, behavior

management, and relationships with students. Teachers are also responsible for executing others' decisions.

7. Teacher Leaders—Among the faculty at a school are teachers whose experience, knowledge, or influence gives them ability, authority, or position to make decisions for other teachers. These teachers may lead grade-level or curriculum areas, participate on special committees, or influence decision-making in other ways.

8. Counselors—Students often go to counselors to ask questions, seek advice, and talk to when they need a supportive adult in school. While they often guide student decision-making with classes or life after high school, counselors may also help students make decisions about life in general.

9. Assistant Principal—Many schools principals need assistants to guide behavior management, budgeting, staff supervision, curriculum, and other areas. They affect students by doling out punishments and rewards; guiding student activities; and in other ways.

10. Principal/HeadMaster—The commonly acknowledged "leader" of a school is responsible for most areas of school operations, including many of the assistant principal roles listed above. They also publicly represent the school; mediate conflicts among students, staff, parents, and community members; and interact with district, state, and federal authorities.

11. District Administration—Officials on the district level administer programs, funds, rules and regulations given to them by their superiors. In some states districts are simply counties (Maryland) or large regions. New York City has more than 10 districts. District offices may also be known as a local education agency, or LEA.

12. District Superintendent—The leader of a given area or group of schools, superintendents are often the first elected official in the chain of decision-making affecting students. Sometimes they are appointed by the district school board or city mayor. They act as the figurehead and authority of all education-related issues within their physical area of authority.

13. District School Board—These elected officials get recommendations from the public and the superintendent to deliver their range of decision-making authority. They set the budget and agenda of schools, assign students to schools, make rules and policies, set learning standards, and more.

14. Regional Administration—These are in-between organizations that may offer professional development, administrative guidance, or funding to districts

student voice in schools

and local schools. These offices have different names, including Educational Service Districts (Washington); BOCEs (New York); or Regional Service Centers (Texas).

15. State Administration—These officials are responsible for administering federal and state programs designed to meet the goals of schools. Also known as the state education agency or department of education. In several states this is the Office of Superintendent of Public Administration.

16. State Education Leader—The state education leader may be elected or appointed; they may also work equally with the state school board and governor, or independently. They are responsible for guiding the implementation of the rules, regulations, laws, budgets, and programs of the state legislature; in some states, the governor; and the federal government. This person may be called the Chief Education Officer, or the Superintendent of Public Instruction (SPI).

17. State School Board—An elected group of officials that overseas all schools and ensures the state's adherence to federal rules and regulations. Students can be meaningfully involved as full voting members elected by their peers are responsible for a full slate of activities, issues, and outcomes.

18. Governor/State Legislature/State Supreme Court—The state-level officials who are responsible for setting state priorities and funding for education, as well as ensuring local, state, and federal compliance with education laws.

19. U.S. Secretary of Education—The individual official responsible for setting and implementing the President's education agenda. Operates the Department of Education, a federal agency responsible for administering the budgets, rules, and regulations of the Secretary of Education and the Congress.

20. U.S. Representatives and U.S. Senators—Elected officials responsible for setting the President's educational policy recommendations into motion, in addition to supplementing their states' policy with additional funding.

21. U.S. Supreme Court Justices—These individuals are appointed to make sure schools comply with the Constitution and Bill of Rights.

22. U.S. President—The elected official responsible for setting national educational priorities affecting all public schools.

29

Clarify Roles in Student Voice Activities

1. Be sure your whole group (committee, office, school, or agency) understands why you're engaging Student Voice and share similar expectations.

2. Involve students from the beginning and make sure their contributions are valued.

3. Consider pairing student members with adult members in a mutual mentorship relationship so questions can be easily answered.

4. Provide orientation opportunities for new members of any age.

5. Involve students in planning of all sorts, including meetings, events, curriculum, recruitment, etc.

6. Create job descriptions for all members of all ages.

7. Communicate directly with students via phone, text, email, etc.

8. Contact all members to remind them of meetings.

9. After any classes, events, meetings, etc. ask students for help adjusting your expectations.

student voice in schools

CRITICAL QUESTIONS FOR STUDENTS

★ Do you know where Student Voice is supposed to change things?

★ Do you know how Student Voice can affect schools, education, and specific things?

★ Who are you trying to share Student Voice with?

★ Will Student Voice activities be all work, or is there fun involved too?

★ Are meetings mandatory for you to attend?

★ What do adults expect of Student Voice? Is that more or less work?

★ Do your friends share your concerns, or are you speaking for yourself?

student voice in schools

Focusing Student Voice

Student Voice can be engaged in a lot of ways. As I read studies from more than four decades of research, I found six major focuses.

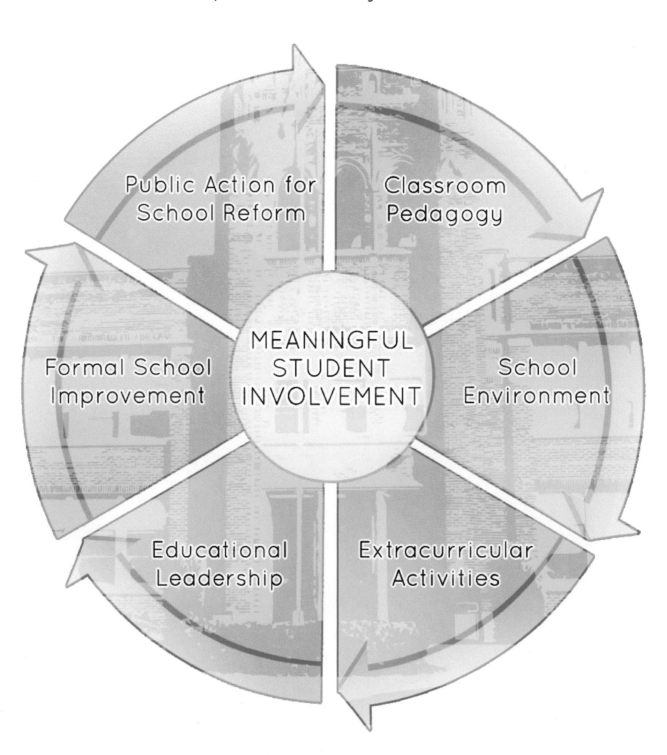

Public Action for School Reform

Classroom Pedagogy

Formal School Improvement

MEANINGFUL STUDENT INVOLVEMENT

School Environment

Educational Leadership

Extracurricular Activities

Focusing Student Voice

Classroom Pedagogy—This is the place where most teaching, learning, and assessment should happen in schools. Teachers study, practice, and build on their teaching skills, and Meaningful Student Involvement can help their professional practice.

School Environment —The environment for teaching and learning is determined by the climate and culture of the school. Meaningful Student Involvement can make many things better, including relationships between students, teacher and staff behavior, and the interactions between students and teachers.

Extracurricular Activities—Student government, clubs, sports, and any other activity not directed by classroom teaching happens in extracurricular activities. Meaningful Student Involvement can make out-of-classroom learning more effective in every way.

Education Leadership—Building principals, local and state boards of education, education agency staff, and federal politicians fall into this category. Meaningful Student Involvement can better consult, negotiate, and drive these school decisions towards effectiveness.

Formal School Improvement—Every kind of public school in the United States has to have a formal school improvement plan. Integrating Meaningful Student Involvement throughout this process can lead to better schools that help for both students and adults.

Public Action for School Reform—Students around the world are asserting their voices into the national dialogue about education transformation, public school privatization, and other essential conversations. Meaningful Student Involvement positions them as leaders of leading student organizing, participating in community-led school reform, and active movements to change education.

Meaningful Student Involvement

How can Student Voice be viewed as sustainably and realistically important? Meaningful Student Involvement is a framework that fosters those student/adult partnerships.

All Student Voice Can Be Meaningful

How meaningful can student voice be? Following are a bunch of powerful, interesting, and exciting things all schools can do to meaningfully involve all student voice! Working together as partners, students and adults in schools can create, sustain, and expand on these actions to make powerful learning for everyone.

1. **Make School Meaningful For ALL Students**—This means that all students in all grades in all schools experience meaningful involvement as a practical part of everyday in school. No more passive teaching or tokenistic involvement. Instead, every student should have student-driven learning, Student-Adult Partnerships, peer-driven conflict resolution and interactive learning conducted in school everyday. Everyday classroom learning can hold all the activity once provided by student councils, and new action can meaningfully involve students!

2. **End Tokenism**—There should be no single seats for students on committees, at conferences, or in education agency meetings. Instead, all school decision-making, including committees, should have students on board as full partners. Meeting techniques should be engaging, and include equal numbers of students and adults as well as full representative power.

3. **Let Students Drive Learning**—Leading their own learning activities already happens for students in some "alternative" schools. Let's make this practice normative in all schools. All K-12 students can co-design their own individual academic programs with adults. Those experiences can be educational and democratic processes. Instead of seeing the situation as, "handing over the keys to the car" to a 16-year-old, student-driven learning can happen for everyone.

4. **Use Restorative Justice In Schools**—Adults in schools can learn to use school rules as things that students can learn from without punitive punishment for any learner. Schools can engage students and adults together in making the rules and figuring out what happens when students break the rules.

5. **Build Democracy In Schools Together**—When student voice is really engaged, it happens from kindergarten through high school graduation. Adults in schools build on what students already know and add to it, instead of pretending students don't know anything. In kindergarten learners can facilitate peer-to-peer conflict resolution, personal decision-making and democratic group

student voice in schools

learning experiences; by forth, fifth and sixth grades students can conduct original research on their schools, complete regular self- and teacher-evaluations, and participate in building-wide decision-making activities; by high school young people should have established clear and equitable relationships with adults throughout schools in order to participate in full student/adult partnerships.

6. Hold Adults Accountable Too—For a long time, adults have measured student achievement in schools without students having any say. More so, it has been completely out of the question for students to measure teacher performance. Students can provide essential feedback on teaching habits, teacher communication, and other parts of teaching. Reciprocal accountability is the future of all schools.

7. Go For A Full-Court Press—All student expression, whether positive, negative or otherwise, must be allowed space and opportunity within schools, and be used towards teaching and learning. By embracing diverse student voice, educators can embrace the potential of learning led by students and learn new ways to relate to, teach, and encourage themselves and everyone in our communities.

8. Emphasize Equity, Not Equality—Well-meaning adults promoting student voice in schools generally assume that all student involvement should be completely equal to adult involvement. However, the most powerful road to take is student/adult equity. Equity is about fairness in schools, equality of access in learning, recognizing inequalities throughout education and taking steps to address them. It is about changing school culture and structure to ensure all student voice has a place, instead of just students who can act like adults.

9. Make Meaning From Life—Every class should be based in students everyday life experiences, as well materials that prepare them for their futures. This makes the ideas, experiences, wisdom and knowledge young people have important. It can position their voices importantly throughout schools.

WAYS ADULTS CAN SUPPORT STUDENT VOICE

★ Offer guidance and moral support.

★ Arrange for students to receive classroom credit for what they learn through Student Voice activities.

★ Make connections with other supportive adults in your school or education agency.

★ Recruit students to recruit other students.

★ Provide access to tools like the Internet, printers, telephones, etc.

★ Be a school-sanctioned sponsor for a student-led campaign.

★ Share your wisdom and experience.

★ Allow students to make mistakes and find answers for themselves.

★ Make sure student activities are safe and appropriate.

★ Provide training on issues and actions that can change schools.

★ Provide transportation to other schools, education agencies, and other locations.

★ Be an advocate for Student Voice in places where students aren't usually in attendance, but should be.

★ Communicate with parents and other adults in school systems.

student voice in schools

The Ladder Of Student Involvement

Sometimes well-meaning adults can make students feel like they are less-than adults when sharing student voice. This happens all kinds of ways. For a long time, the only formal position every young person holds in society is that of student: Every young person is a learner who attends school in order to meet society's expectations of them. That has changed. Today, young people increasingly have more important positions, including that of decision-makers, planners, researchers, and more. The following *Ladder of Student Involvement in Schools* was created to encourage students and adults to examine *why* and *how* students participate throughout schools. Think of specific activities students are involved in, and measure them against this tool.

It is important to recognize that the Ladder is not meant to represent the whole school at once. Instead, it represents each specific instance of student involvement. That means that rather than say a whole classroom is rung 4, several students could be experiencing that they are at that rung while others are experiencing that they're at rung 6. For a long time, determining which rung a student is at was left to perception and position: If an adult believed the students on their committee were at rung 6, and the students believed they were at rung 8, they simply agreed to disagree.

Ladder of Student Involvement

8. Youth/Adult Equity

7. Completely Youth-Driven

6. Youth/Adult Equality

Meaningful
Student
Involvement

---

5. Youth Consulted

4. Youth Informed

---

3. Tokenism

2. Decoration

Traditional
Student
Involvement

1. Manipulation

student voice in schools

You're Experiencing Student/Adult Equity If...

- ☐ Students and adults acknowledge and use everyone's unique abilities.
- ☐ There is a 40/60 split of power, or 20/80 split when it's appropriate.
- ☐ Students and adults are recognized for their impact and ownership of the outcomes.

You're Experiencing Student-Led Action If...

- ☐ Students plan, implement, and evaluate all activities.
- ☐ Adults are not in positions of authority.
- ☐ Students are fully accountable for the outcomes of activities.
- ☐ Students control the budget, curriculum, and training for themselves and others.

You're Experiencing Student-Adult Equality If...

- ☐ Adults and students have a 50/50 split of authority, obligation, and commitment.
- ☐ All activities are co-led and equally represented by students and adults.
- ☐ Students have rights and responsibilities that are equal to adults.

You're Experiencing Students Consulting Adults If...

- ☐ Students have a voice without any decision-making authority while adults design, plan, consider, and move activities.
- ☐ Adults maintain full authority and final say over the outcomes.
- ☐ Students are responsible for individual parts of an activity while adults are responsible for the outcomes.

You're Experiencing Students Informing Adults If...

- ☐ Adults ask students what they think without giving them a formal role in decision-making in schools.
- ☐ Students participate in forums, online conversations, or other places where adults determine what gets responded to or acted upon.

You're Experiencing Student Tokenism If...

- ☐ Adults refer to a student representative as "Our Student".
- ☐ If students are sitting at the table with adults with no real ability but shown as great examples of Student Voice.
- ☐ If one student is expected to represent all students.

student voice in schools

You're Experiencing Student as Decorations If...

☐ Adults treat students like their presence is all that is necessary without their action or input.

☐ If students are asked to attend adult activities without any training or preparation.

You're Experiencing Student Manipulation If...

☐ Students are forced to attend whether or not they want to.

☐ If credit, money, or acceptance are used as levers to assure student participation.

Roger Hart, a sociologist for UNICEF who conceived of a Ladder for children's participation in environmental organizations, originally intended the first three rungs to represent forms of *non*-participation. However, while the first rung generally represents the nature of all student involvement in schools with the threat of "attend or fail", there are more roles for students than ever before throughout the education system.

My research shows that high levels of participation are apparent in schools— they just aren't widespread. Rungs 6, 7, and 8 generally represent "student/ adult partnerships", or intentional arrangements designed to foster authentic student engagement in schools.

It's important to stay hopeful about the educational system.

Today, students are increasingly engaged as researchers, planners, teachers, evaluators, decision-makers, and advocates. With this knowledge in mind, the rungs of the Ladder can help students and adults identify how students are currently involved in schools, and give them goals to aspire towards.

65 Ways Students Can Make School Meaningful

With all the talk about how schools need to change and all the different actions students can take to change schools, figuring out where to start can be hard! The following list of actions students can take to change schools includes all sorts of different ways students can help schools become better places to attend and to learn.

1. **Identify An Adult Ally In School.** Find an adult in your school who is safe, supportive, and empowering. Talk with them about being there for you as you work to change your own learning and your school, and ask if they'll be an adult ally to you.

2. **Have A Real Conversation With A Teacher.** Ask a teacher what they want to see happen to make schools better places. Have real, frank, open, and honest conversations with other adults, too, each focused on what they want to see happen. Find out if they see any role for students in making those things happen.

3. **Propose A Student-Adult Partnership Program In Your School.** Offer a group of students who are willing to talk openly with teachers and administrators about how they think schools should change, and hold dialogue opportunities for students and adults to talk together.

student voice in schools

4. **Lead Other Students In Taking Action.** Create a formal or informal group for students who want to make your school a better place. Meet regularly, make plans, and take action.

5. **Have A Mixer.** Host a school improvement mixer for students and adults in schools who are concerned with creating better schools to encourage student-adult partnerships.

6. **Meet With School Leaders.** Call for a meeting with the principal for students to highlight the concerns and recommendations you have for school.

7. **Support Non-Tokenized Meetings.** Talk to adults about meaningfully involving young people in meetings, and consider declining to attend meetings where only one highly involved student is invited.

8. **Hang Out At School.** Find an adult ally who will make their classroom a comfortable, safe, and affirming place so students can "hang-out."

9. **Ask An Adult For Help.** If they know about computers, ask them to assist you. If they understand diversity, ask them to teach you.

10. **Recognize Adult Involvement.** Don't assume that just because someone is an adult that they enjoy school. Help them appreciate it by giving credit where its due.

11. **Hold Adults Accountable For Their Mistakes, Challenges, And Failures.** Be honest and forthright with adults, while supporting their efforts to improve.

12. **Treat Adults As Individuals.** One adult cannot represent all adults, and each must learn how to represent themselves. Teach them. Be the change you wish to see. Speak to adults with respect, and avoid interrupting other youth or adults.

13. **Watch The Change Happen.** Hold a movie night and discussion for students and adults either at your school or in your community.

14. **Teach A Teacher.** Do you know things about technology, the community, or other topics you think that teachers, parents, community members, or other adults can learn? Hold a student-led professional development session and invite adults from throughout your school to

student voice in schools

attend. Create a tight program, identify real learning goals, and facilitate good learning for everyone involved.

15. Start A Resource Library. Gather materials from across the Internet that will help you develop a successful campaign to change your school, and inspire you to do more. Share those links with your friends, parents, teachers, and others. Include books, websites, and organizations working on school improvement, student organizing and activism, and youth power.

16. Teach Other Students About Education. Hold workshops and teach-ins for your friends to learn how schools need to change and what they can do to make a difference. Build on what they already know.

17. Teach About School Change. Work with a teacher to co-design a lesson plan for students, parents, and the community about education reform and student involvement.

18. Get Listed. Create a listing of all opportunities for involvement in your school and community.

19. Conduct A Teach-In On School Reform For Students and Adults. Teaching students, parents, and community members what school reform is and how it happens is an important way to get more voices at the table.

20. Write A Curriculum. Do you know a better way to teach something? Propose to a teacher to write and test a lesson plan or even a week-long curriculum and ask if you can test it in their class.

21. Work Inside Or Outside The School. Work in your school to change your school whenever possible, but work out-of-school to change your school if you must. Find a local nonprofit that will host your gatherings and provide you with assistance, if you want it.

22. Go Citywide. Have a town meeting or school forum for everyone at your school. Invite parents and community members.

23. Be A Connector. Are a lot of teachers in your school building from neighborhoods outside of your school's immediate community? Offer to teachers to serve as a neighborhood connector by introducing them to the resources you use locally, especially after school program staff and nonprofit leaders.

24. **Connect The Dots.** Connect with students in your city or state who want to involve students meaningfully, both in your school and others, and around the community.

25. **Engage Voters.** Support political candidates for local, state, and national office who make listening and working with students in schools a priority.

26. **Follow Some Leaders.** Serve in a community-based campaign that is led by other students and community leaders.

27. **Get Some Money.** Raise funds for a student-led organization focusing on school issues locally.

28. **Look To Your Community.** Actively support youth-led organizations in your community, and encourage them to address education reform.

29. **Start A Policy Change Campaign.** Want to create long-lasting, effective changes that will affect every student in your state? Target a state law affecting schools that you want to see changed and work towards changing it. Try partnering with education advocacy organizations, and if that doesn't work, form your own student-driven coalition for school change.

30. **Talk To Policy-Makers.** District school board makers, state legislators, and Congress members are responsible for making education laws in every state, including setting funding priorities and academic achievement goals. These elected officials need to know students are concerned, too.

31. **Learn About Policy Change.** Advocate for a specific school policy change, including curriculum, cell phone usage, truancy and attendance, etc., and call for it to change.

32. **Join School Boards When Possible.** If that's not possible, join the student advisory board. Today, an increasing number of students have roles, and you can share this information with your local board, too.

33. **Conduct Research Studies.** Use participatory action research in your school to identify what needs to change and how it can happen, as well as who should be involved.

34. **Research Students' Perspectives On Schools.** Students' opinions change from clique to clique, grade to grade, school to school -

student voice in schools

but in many policy-makers' eyes, students are simply another constituent group. Research a large swath of students' perspectives across your entire school, district, or state, and share those results with education decision-makers who should hear them.

35. **Evaluate The Education System.** Call for your school to have regular student evaluations of themselves, teachers, administrators, and classes that influence performance evaluations, contracts, and hiring.

36. **Find The Truth.** Survey students and adults and parents in your school and present the results to the community, including the school board and others.

37. **Be An Advocate For Student Voice At Any School Meeting.** Advertise any public meeting to students, and encourage adults to make sure students are at the table whenever your school is making choices about students.

38. **Post Your Concerns.** Make students concerns visible in your school by posting them in your classroom, sharing them at meetings where adults are, and posting them on the Internet.

39. **Write Letters Of Concern.** Work with other students to develop a letter writing campaign that informs principals, district and state school board members, the newspaper, and elected officials about student concerns regarding education.

40. **Be Real.** Be consistent and clear about your expectations of adults in your school, including how they treat students and what the outcomes should be.

41. **Have A Call-In.** Arrange for a radio station to sponsor a call-in show led by students that allows them to talk about their concerns about school.

42. **Get Artistic.** Meet with students in your school who are particularly artistic, and develop a proposal with them for your building's leader to create art around the building focused on school reform. This might include icons painted on hallways throughout the building, or a mural summarizing students' visions for schools.

43. **See The Future.** Create a school-wide vision for student involvement and voice that includes adults and students.

student voice in schools

44. Spread The Word. Create a newsletter, website, or Facebook group to share students' concerns about their school and education.

45. Be An Advocate. Call for student involvement and student/adult partnerships throughout the education system.

46. Meet With School Board. Let elected district school directors know that students care about their schools and their education by attending school board meetings and presenting issues students care about. Ask directors if you can meet with them individually to present your concerns, as well.

47. Learn About Classroom Teaching. Work with your friends to study and learn about effective teaching, and offer feedback to teachers in an accessible, non-threatening way.

48. Be A Teacher Coach. After forming a student/adult partnership with an adult ally in your school, offer to coach them by providing regular feedback in an appropriate fashion after class or after school. Share your insights about how they can teach better, manage more effectively, or effectively involve other students in class.

49. Provide Voluntary Evaluations Of Teacher Performance. Find out which teachers in your school want student-led evaluations of their performance, and lead a small cadre into their class during study hall periods to assess them. Then share those results with the teacher.

50. Be A Friend. Be a real, active, and engaged friend to adults in schools. They need allies too.

51. Respect Adults Like You Do Students. Don't expect more from adults than you do students and don't interpret for other students what they can say for themselves.

52. Give Yourself Some Feedback. Have students self-evaluate themselves, their classes, and their teachers, and provide those results to teachers.

53. Push For Reality. When teachers assign you tasks to

student voice in schools

create imaginary situations or participate in "mock" activities like government law-making or elections, take on assignment topics that address real school issues. Do legitimate work and apply your classroom learning to real-life scenarios that affect you every day.

54. **Create A Student-Led School Reform Group.** Work with your peers to identify, define, focus, and organize a student-led school reform campaign for your school or in schools across your community. Use traditional protest tactics to demand meaningful student involvement throughout schools, and the types of reforms students think should happen.

55. **Involve Non-Traditionally Engaged Students.** Listen specifically to students whose voices are seldom heard in schools, including students who are minority, low-income, have low grades, or don't interact with their peers.

56. **Share The Wealth.** Arrange resources for students who would not otherwise be able to participate in school activities, including transportation, permission, and childcare.

57. **Refuse Inequitable Rewards.** Work against unfair opportunities for students that are based only on academic performance, attendance, race, gender, etc.

58. **Support The Whole Student.** Sponsor a support group for students who face particular difficulties such as parents' divorce, violence, etc.

59. **Call For New Roles.** Encourage your school to involve students as advisers to the principal, classroom consultants, interns, apprentices, and activities staff.

60. **Become An Interviewer.** Call for schools to include students in hiring adults at your school, including staff, teachers, and administrators.

61. **Self-Monitor Behavior.** Encourage your school building leadership to consider adopting a student-led conflict resolution program such as a peer leaders, a restorative justice program, or a student court.

62. **Create Expectations.** Ask your teachers to co-create group expectations and norms for classroom behavior and action.

student voice in schools

63. **Get Students On Board!** No decisions about students should be made without students, and getting students onto school building-level, district, and state committees and boards is an important way to involve students in school decision-making.

64. **Build The Web.** Connect with students across the U.S., Canada, Australia, the UK, on the African Continent, across Europe, and in other countries around the world where there are powerful and effective student voice initiatives. Link to them, share their work, and share with them as much as you can.

65. **Volunteer For Student-Led Organizations.** Student-led organizations want adults to be allies.

If you have worked your way through these 65 items, you have transformed your school!

student voice in schools

50 Ways Adults Can Make School Meaningful

The following things that adults throughout schools can do to support, empower, and involve students throughout the education system. Adults outside schools can support students these ways too, and work to make sure adults in schools are doing them.

1. **Have A Real Conversation With A Student.** Ask a student what they want to do find out how you can help make that happen.

2. **Actively Support Student-Led Action.** However possible, including working with students out-of-school to accomplish their goals in education.

3. **Start A Resource Library.** Inspire students to make change with materials or link collections. Include books, websites, and organizations working on democracy, social change, schools, and youth power.

4. **Use Active Learning Methods.** Teach students about education, including service learning and constructivism. Build on what they already know.

5. **Develop A Student-Adult Partnership Program.** In your school where students and educators can actually discuss school together.

6. **Create a Student Voice Center.** Use your school for students to become involved in changing their school and communities.

7. **Use Participatory Action Research In Your Classroom.** Students can use PAR to establish substantial action in your school.

8. **Be An Advocate For Students At School Meetings.** Make sure students are at the table whenever your school is making choices about students.

9. **Focus On Critical Thinking.** Create classroom lesson plans that actively engage students in critical thinking about education and action that changes schools.

10. **Make Student Voice Visible.** Make students concerns visible in your school by posting them in your classroom and sharing them at meetings where adults are.

11. **Promote Structural Change.** Sponsor a letter with students to the administration about student issues.

12. **Respect Students As You Do Adults.** Don't expect more from students than you do adults and don't interpret for students what they can say for themselves.

13. **Bring Students In As Teachers.** Co-design a lesson plan with students about education reform and student involvement.

14. **Amplify Under-engaged Voices.** Listen specifically to students whose voices are seldom heard in schools, including students who are minority, low-income, have low grades, or don't interact with their peers.

15. **Connect The Dots.** Host an activity for students and educators to encourage student-adult partnerships.

16. **Position Students For Action.** Engage students as classroom consultants, interns, apprentices, and activities staff.

17. **Make Expectations Obvious.** Be consistent and clear about your expectations of students in your classroom.

18. **Make Spaces For Student Voice To Sound Out.** Team up with students to have a town meeting or school forum for everyone at your school.

19. **Create Networks With Students.** Identify and network with students in your school who are concerned about their school.

20. **Build Support For The Movement.** Connect with other adult allies who want to involve students meaningfully, both in your school and others, and around the community.

21. **Let Students Hire Adults.** Include students in hiring adults at your school, including staff, teachers, and administrators.

22. **Support Engagement For Under-Resourced Students.** Arrange resources for students who would not otherwise be able to participate in school activities, including transportation, permission, and childcare.

student voice in schools

23. Represent Student Voice At The Ballot Box. Support political candidates for local, state, and national office who make listening and working with young people a priority.

24. Broadcast Student Voice. Arrange for a radio station to sponsor a call-in show led by students that allows them to talk about their concerns about school.

25. Meet With Leaders. Arrange an meeting with the principal for students to highlight the concerns and recommendations they have for school.

26. Go Big. Create a school-wide vision for student involvement and voice that includes adults and students.

27. Get Into Standing Opportunities. Serve on an advisory board or board of directors for a student-led effort.

28. Stand Strong When Necessary. Refuse to attend meetings where students are not invited or where you cannot bring students with you.

29. Get Real. Be a real, active, and engaged friend to students.

30. Level The Field. Discourage unfair opportunities for students based on academic performance, attendance, race, gender, etc.

31. Think Wide. Create student-led experiences in your classroom and throughout your school.

32. Create Good Space. Make your classroom a comfortable, safe, and affirming place so students can "hang-out."

33. Support The Word Getting Spread. Help students create an online newsletter, or work with your school newspaper, to share students' concerns about their school and education.

34. Identify Current Opportunities. Help students create a listing of all opportunities for student voice in your school and community.

35. Advocate For Student Self-Evaluation. Call for your school to have regular student evaluations of themselves, teachers, administrators, and classes that influence performance evaluations, contracts, and hiring.

36. Ask A Student For Help. If they know about computers, ask them to assist you. If they understand diversity, ask them to teach you.

37. Support Students For Real. Sponsor a support group for students who face particular difficulties such as parents' divorce, violence, etc.

38. Get Money. Raise funds for a student-led organization focusing on school issues.

39. **Give Money Or Time.** Actively support youth-led organizations in your community, and encourage them to address education reform.

40. **Be Active In The Community.** Join (or form) with students a community task force to address youth issues and coordinate responses in schools.

41. **Train Students.** Prepare students for multiple roles in your school, including learner, teacher, and leader.

42. **Demonstrate Openness.** Ask students' advice on school issues you are wrestling with.

43. **Build Allies.** Start an adult support group to share ideas, concerns, and ways to listen better to students.

44. **Recognize Student Voice.** Don't assume that just because someone is a student that they enjoy school. Help them appreciate it by giving class credit or through other meaningful recognition.

45. **Inject Student Voice In Professional Settings.** Include students in the membership and on committees in professional education organizations.

46. **Hold Students Accountable For Their Mistakes And Challenges.** Be honest and forthright with young people, and support their efforts to improve.

47. **Treat Students As Individuals.** One student cannot represent all students, and must learn how to represent themselves. Teach them.

48. **Act Right.** Speak to students with respect, and avoid interrupting students.

49. **Begin At The Beginning.** Involve students from the beginning of class by having them create a list of their own expectations for the climate of the classroom through the end by having them conduct self-, class-, and teacher-evaluations.

50. **Get Loud.** Become a system-wide advocate by continuing your movement towards Meaningful Student Involvement by calling for student voice throughout the education system, and by offering yourself and your classroom as a resource consistently.

Working together, students and adults can successfully transform all schools everywhere for all students!

student voice in schools

Action Plan for Student Voice

	YES	NO	N/A
Step 1—Define what you want to change about your school. Learn how it works, what happens, what causes it, and what it will take to change it.			
Step 2—Name why Student Voice should be engaged. No matter what area of schools, have a good reason.			
Step 3—Assess where involvement happens right now. Identify successes, challenges, and failures honestly.			
Step 4—Name how involvement can happen. The area you've chose to transform has specific ways. Identify them.			
Step 5—Engage diverse students. Whatever your school transformation work is, bring in people you don't know.			
Step 6—Build community. Don't just work together; learn together, play together, and change together.			
Step 7—Identify clear goals. Ensure that Student Voice is loud and clear by naming when, how, where, and why change will happen.			
Step 8—Provide opportunities for students and adults to learn together. Make it personal and let them connect.			
Step 9—Foster real student/adult partnerships in action. Provide training, share materials, and give ideas.			
Step 10—Make a sustainable plan for Student Voice. Have impact beyond yourself by using strategy to change the school system.			
Step 11—Reflect and Celebrate along the way. Changing schools is challenging for anyone. Look back and what you've done, examine successes, challenges, and failures, and celebrate that you're taking action!			

STEPS TO DETERMINE SCHOOL PRIORITIES - WHAT YOU WANT TO CHANGE ABOUT YOUR SCHOOL

Determine what's most important in your school or education setting by prioritizing and creating an action plan to address those issues. To prioritize, follow these steps:

1. Brainstorm a list of issues in your school and throughout the education system.

2. Give everyone in your group 50 points apiece.

3. Ask everyone to assign points to each issue according to their importance, giving the most points to the issues you feel are most important. Add up points given to each issue.

4. Rewrite your list in issue of importance, with the ones getting the most points at the top.

5. Declare the top issues as your school's priorities for Student Voice! And then follow the Action Planning steps for a step-by-step process for acting on your priorities.

Resources

The following are websites, organizations, and publications you can rely on for more information about student voice.

SoundOut

soundout.org

Promoting student voice in schools. Operating since 2001, SoundOut has worked with more than 300 K-12 schools across the US and Canada. We provide training, tools, and technical assistance about student voice, authentic student engagement, and Meaningful Student Involvement. Call (360) 489-9680 or email info@soundout.org.

All the research mentioned in this guide, along with best practices, stories, and other resources, can be found online at soundout.org/publications.html. Like us on Facebook at fb.com/SoundOut or follow us on Twitter at twitter.com/SoundOutorg

UP for Learning/Youth and Adults Transforming Schools Together

yatst.com

UP for Learning/YATST is a network of Vermont schools dedicated to fostering schools where learning is engaging and youth are empowered through an action research process. Call (802) 472-5127 or email info@yatst.com

Student Voice Matters

studentvoicematters.org

Youth on Board is working to build a broad-based movement across the US to promote student voice and strengthen student teacher relationships in the classroom in an effort to create supportive, equitable, and student-centered school environments. Call (617) 741-1242 or email info@youthonboard.org

Student Voice

stuvoice.org

Student Voice strives to create an international network of empowered students by providing them with the tools they need to use their voice in policy discussions. Email stuvoice1@gmail.com

What Kids Can Do

whatkidscando.org

What Kids Can Do documents the good work of young people as well as sponsoring our own projects. Call (401) 247-7665 or email info@whatkidscando.org

student voice in schools

Adam Fletcher is an internationally-recognized, award-winning expert in youth engagement. Through SoundOut and The Freechild Project, he has worked with more than 1,000,000 people in schools across the United States and Canada. Today, he contracts with around the world as a public speaker, facilitator, trainer, freelance writer, and consultant for organizations, and serves as a professional coach for individuals. Learn more about him at adamfletcher.net.

Also by Adam Fletcher:

The Guide to Student Voice 2nd Edition (2014)

Guide to Students on School Boards (2014)

A Short Guide to Holistic Youth Development (2014)

A Short Introduction to Youth Engagement (2014)

Ending Discrimination Against Young People (2013)

The Freechild Project Guide to Youth-Driven Programming (2013)

SoundOut Student Voice Curriculum (2013)

The Freechild Project Youth Action Guide (2013)

Meaningful Student Involvement Deep Assessment (2013)

Student Voice and Bullying: A SoundOut Focus Paper (2012)

The Freechild Project Youth Engagement Workshop Guide (2011)

The Freechild Project Youth Voice Toolkit (2010)

Washington Youth Voice Handbook (2007)

The Freechild Project Guide to Social Change Led By and With Young People (2007)

Meaningful Student Involvement: Guide to Students as Partners in School Change (2005)

The Freechild Project Guide to Cooperative Games for Social Change (2005)

Stories of Meaningful Student Involvement (2004)

Meaningful Student Involvement Research Guide (2004)

Meaningful Student Involvement Idea Guide for Schools (2003)

Firestarter Youth Empowerment Curriculum (2001)

For more information or to order visit adamfletcher.net/books

CPSIA information can be obtained
at www.ICGtesting.com
Printed in the USA
BVHW021924300621
610919BV00001B/1